B & M Potterycrafts.

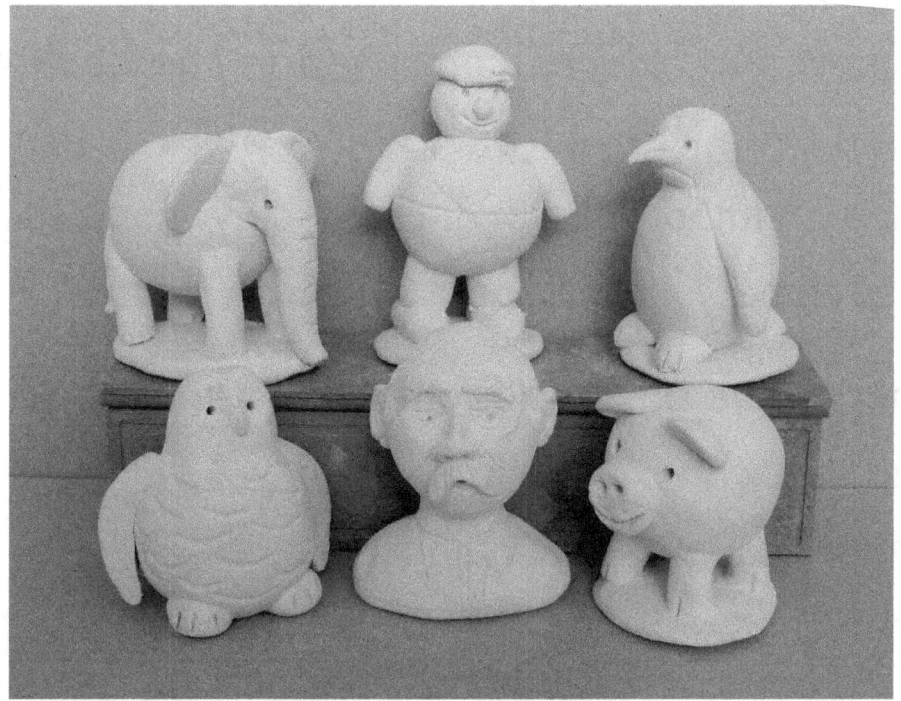

Thumb Pot Models.

Create the **Double Thumb Pot** models shown on this page by following step by step, easy to understand, instructions supported by still photos at each stage.

Thumb pot elephant.

Tweedle Dum and Tweedle Dee.

Penguin.

Olly the Owl.

Head and Shoulders.

Pig.

Brian Rollins.

Simple thumb/pinch pot modelling.

The animals and figures contained in the book were developed over the years and have been used to introduce an important branch of clay modelling to students namely **thumb pots** or **pinch pots**.

The figures are built up from simple shapes to which the students can relate, the base shape made using thumb pot techniques.

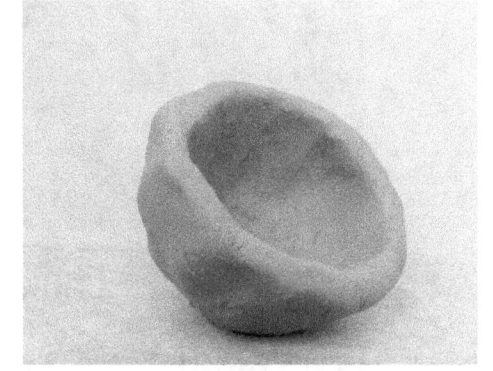

Each project is demonstrated step by step as you work through the text, this is the technique we developed and found most effective in getting our message across over the years, and the objective of each step of the project is shown in the still photos. The step by step approach allows teachers to control the pace of the exercise, helping slower pupils at each stage and handing out the next piece of clay when **all** the pupils are ready.

The most important sheet in each project is the **'Worksheet'** which contains the weight of clay and the templates required to ensure the correct proportions of the models.

Each project has an element of decision making and measurement built into the worksheet with self-

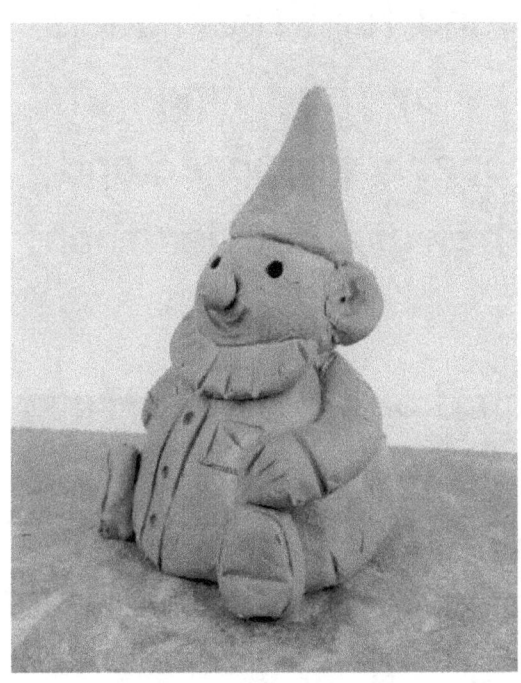

expression encouraged in the decoration and design details applied to each model which becomes an individual creation.

Used regularly the projects will turn Teachers and Classroom Assistants into experienced modellers in clay.

Repeated exposure to the techniques will encourage school staff to design and expand in-house projects. The keys are the weights, dimensions, and shapes. See our **'Thirty Steps to Clay Modelling'** for further information which outlines all the basic skills needed for successful clay modelling projects.

Why Thumb Pots?

This publication is intended to extend the knowledge and stretch the imagination of students who have encountered and enjoyed modelling simple figures and animals in clay.

Using thumb pot techniques allows us to make and fire more substantial models in clay.

If we wish to use pieces of clay and turn the models into pottery we are limited in size by the firing process. Solid pieces of clay, properly prepared and dried cannot be easily fired if they are heavier than 100 grams.

The firing process must be carried out slowly at first allowing the temperature to rise by no more than 100 degrees centigrade per hour giving time for any moisture to escape through the body of the clay as steam. Failure to do this can cause complete shattering of the model.

Piercing holes in the cay with wooden prodders or even drills is one solution but the usual process is to make the models hollow.

When you make the step of hollowing the clay your next limitation is the thickness of the clay, for the same reason, because as the weight limits the escape of steam from the model in firing it stands to reason that the same problem is there in the thickness of the clay walls.

Thumb pot models help us solve part of the problem and generally take two main types, a single thumb pot

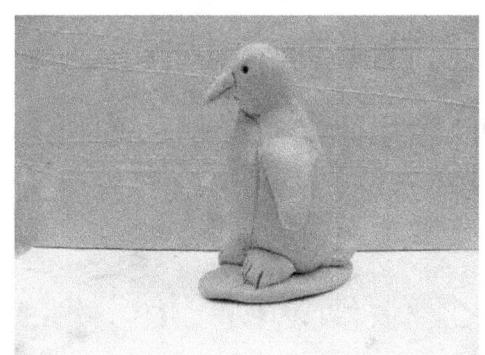

which is an open model and multiple thumb pots in which two or more singles are joined together in an enclosed manner.

Again these multiple pot models need small holes to allow the steam to escape during firing.

Double thumb pot modelling is studied in this project book.

We look into making large and small animal figures and a rounded human shape in Tweedle Dum and Tweedle Dee and explore the creation of human heads.

Some of our figures have a round hollow profile and some have an oval shape as a base for the body

This branch of clay modelling lends itself to all kinds of innovations and our suggestions represent a few for you to expand on and develop, we teach you the basic techniques, the rest is up to you and your imagination.

Preparation.

The Worksheet should be made available to each work group to allow them access to the templates, we have found that one sheet to four pupils is a good balance.

As the sheet can come into contact with wet clay it is recommended that the master is copied and each sheet is sleeved or laminated to avoid clay smudges. Once the sheets are covered they can be kept for future sessions and become a **school resource.**

When we worked with groups the clay was prepared prior to the session.

Preparation consisted of weighing out the pieces and sealing clay for a specific purpose in a plastic bag to keep it moist.

The reasons and techniques for weighing clay are just one of the topics addressed in our on line clay modelling course. Visit our website for details.

www.bmpotterycrafts.co.uk

Clay Modelling Tools.

All the tools can be bought in craft or hobby shops or you can produce cheap alternatives which are just as good and in some cases better and more suitable for use in schools.

Modelling tools shown are the simple tools needed for sculpting small models, most thumb pots and most coil pots.

The paint brush is chosen for its stiff bristles which allow you to rough up the clay to help with cross hatching or obviate the need for cross hatching in some circumstances.

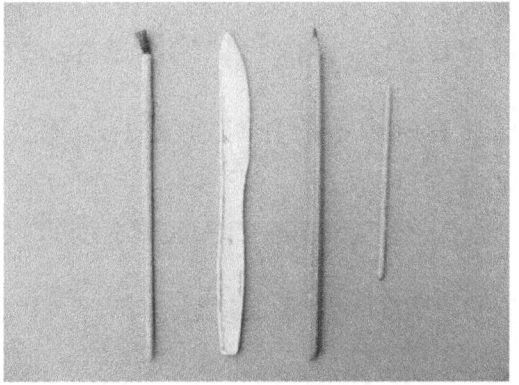

Plastic knives with the serrated edges trimmed using scissors and sharpened on sand paper are a cheap alternative to a potter's fettling knife and more suitable for use by young children. They are used primarily for cutting lengths of clay but can be used as a spatula to smooth joints between pieces of clay.

Pencils or pointed sticks, shown in the picture, are used for adding details such as eyes or hair to models or drawing patterns and designs on pots of all descriptions. The pointed stick shown was made from 3mm thick skewers used in cooking Kebabs. Cut the skewer to the length you need, I made three from one skewer, sharpen one end and round off the other end using sand paper.

The work surface shown is made from 4mm thick, three ply or MDF sheet and is 20cm x 30cm or 15cmx20cm if you are making smaller models.

These tools represent a one off purchase as a central resource for a school to be used by any class as required.

Enjoy your clay modelling.

Brian.

B & M Potterycrafts.

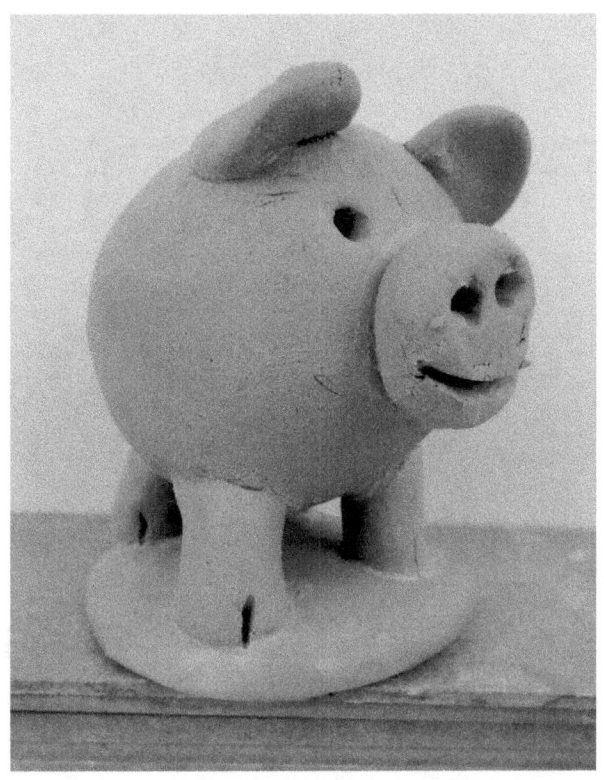

Clay modelling projects.

Double Thumb Pot Pig.

Create the model shown on this cover by following step by step, easy to understand, instructions supported by still photos at each stage.

Brian Rollins.

B & M Potterycrafts.

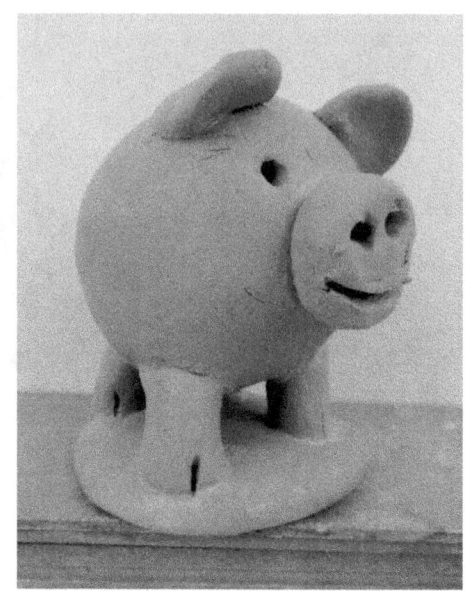

Double Thumb Pot Pig.

Contents and sequence.

Create a single thumb pot.

Make a second thumb pot.

Join two thumb pots.

Make and fit the snout.

Make and fit the ears.

Make and fit the legs.

Make and fit the tail.

Make the base and fit the pig.

Worksheet.

Double thumb pot pig.

Create a single thumb pot.

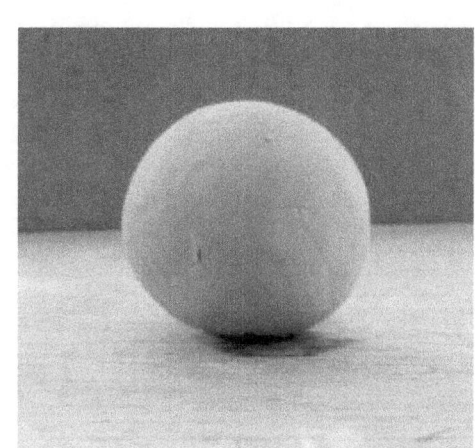

The first part in creating a thumb pot from a ball of clay is to ensure that the ball is round and smooth.

Roll the clay between the palms of your hands, exerting sufficient force to remove any lumps or bumps. Don't be tempted to take the easy route to smooth the clay by rolling it on the wooden work surface as this removes moisture from the clay and could make it too hard for modelling. Any creases or cracks can be smoothed using the fingers. Continue to roll the clay until the surface is smooth and the clay is the desired shape i.e. a ball shape.

The main reasons for this are that if the clay is not smooth before you start to stretch it any cracks will appear as a weakness and the clay will split at those points, to get round this problem check for cracks after each stage of the hollowing and stretching process, smooth out any cracks around the edge with pressure from your fingers.

Please note that if the clay isn't spherical before you start to form the pot you have little chance of finishing with a circular thumb pot.

To start the thumb pot hold the clay in the tips if the fingers of both hands with both thumbs touching the clay, put the thumb nails together until the first

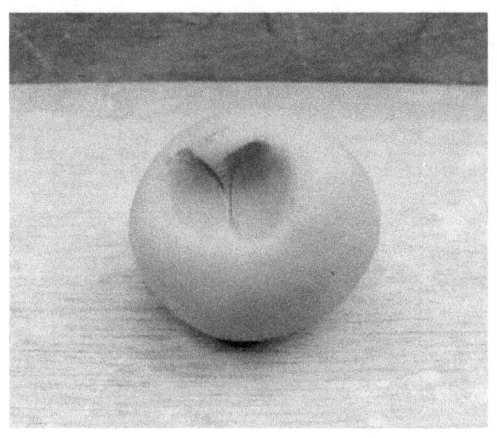

knuckles touch each other. Now press your thumbs firmly into the clay leaving two clear impressions like the ones in the picture.

Turn the clay round and put your thumbs back into the hole and press your thumbs into the clay again, making the hole deeper. You can now use the pressure

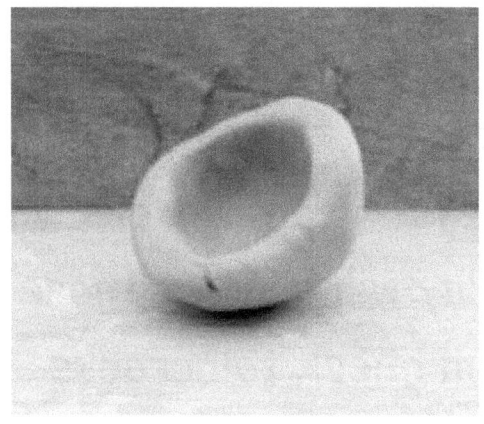

of your thumbs inside the pot against the fingers outside the pot to make the hole deeper and wider, turn the pot round as you gently squeeze the sides of the pot.

At this point measure the diameter of your pot against the template on the worksheet, which is the diameter of the pot that you are aiming for. The overall effect can be likened to a half ball or the top of a mushroom.

Because we are making two thumb pots which have to be joined along the rims these rims need to be thick enough to form a substantial joint. Make sure that the rims are not too thin and that the thickness of the pot sides is carried through to the edge.

Make a second thumb pot.
Repeat the previous section to make a second, identical thumb pot, be sure that you follow the same process so that you will get the same result.

The next activity is to join the two pots along the rims, hold the two pots edge to edge to check that the diameters match and that there is sufficient clay to form a good seal at the joint.

Join two thumb pots.
One tip before we start the joining process, to give a better chance of matching the edges, is to hold each pot in your cupped hand and gently tap the edge on the work surface. This makes the edge level, smooth

and slightly thicker making a good substantial surface ready for crosshatching.

With the point of the knife **crosshatch** both of the edges to be joined and create **slip** on both surfaces by rubbing the brush loaded with water across the crosshatch marks.

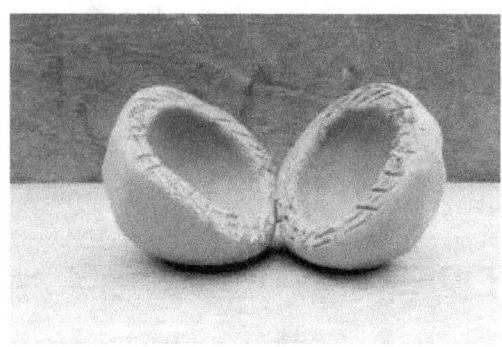 Hold one half of the body in the palm of your hand to support the edges and by holding the knife like a pencil you can use the sharp edge to score marks in the clay. Cut the marks into the surface in one direction, turning the half sphere around until the marks are around the complete circle. Reverse this process to make crosses on the whole surface as shown on the picture.

Repeat this process on the other half sphere before applying slip.

*The creation of **slip** is an important part of joining together two pieces of clay. The water from the brush is rubbed firmly into the clay surface until it turns light grey*

Crosshatching *is one of the keys to joining two pieces of clay. It consists of the scoring the pieces in the areas to be joined. Use the point of the knife to mark clay.*

Creating slip on the crosshatch marks in this manner

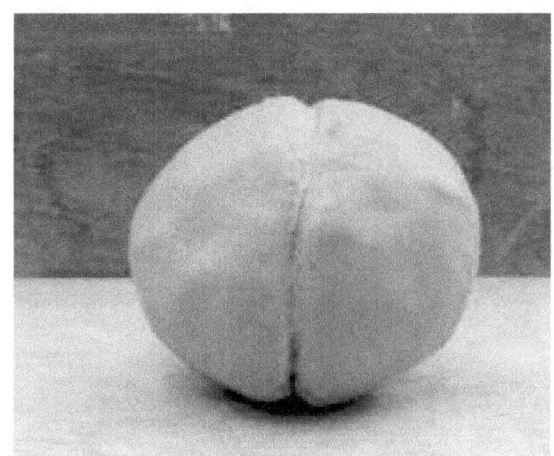

allows water to penetrate the crosshatch marks into the clay surface forming a larger surface area for the water to soften and help to form the slip.

When you have prepared slip on both halves of the body hold one in each hand, bring the two prepared surfaces into contact and press them firmly together with a slight sliding motion across the surfaces to ensure that you get a good bond. The next part of the process is to seal and hide the joint. First, with the tip of your thumb or finger scrape clay from one half - sphere to the other alternating the strokes, one way then the other to give an even distribution. Use the flat surface of the knife blade like a spatula to further smooth and tidy the join.

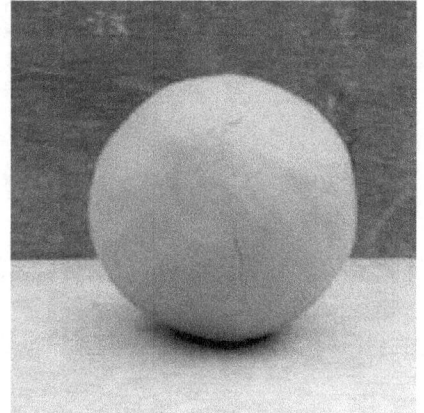

At this stage the pig's body is a ball shaped piece of clay again, in fact it is actually a bubble of air surrounded by clay.

Finally take the hollow ball of clay in the palms of your hands and treat it like a solid ball by rolling it between your palms as you did in preparation, rolling it until it is smooth and free from blemishes. Final smoothing of the bubble of clay can be done on a plastic work surface if a really smooth surface is required.

Make and fit the snout.

Making the snout begins with rolling the clay into a 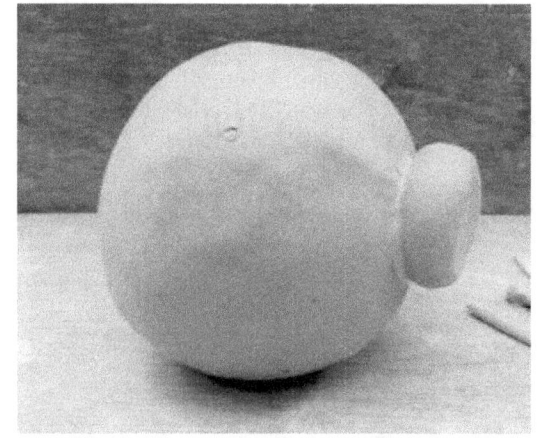 smooth ball and then squashing it slightly with your thumb on the work surface, creating a thick disc. Crosshatch one side of the disc and a similar sized area on the thumb pot. Create slip by rubbing the brush loaded with water across the crosshatched surfaces of the snout and the body, you will notice that the surface goes slightly lighter in colour, this material is your slip.

Support the bubble of clay in the palm of one hand in order to maintain the ball shape and to avoid squashing it and carefully but firmly press the slip on the snout into the slip on the body. The completed shape is shown in the picture.

Make and fit the ears.

.To make two identical ears first roll the clay into a short sausage, mark the middle of the sausage shape with the edge of your knife

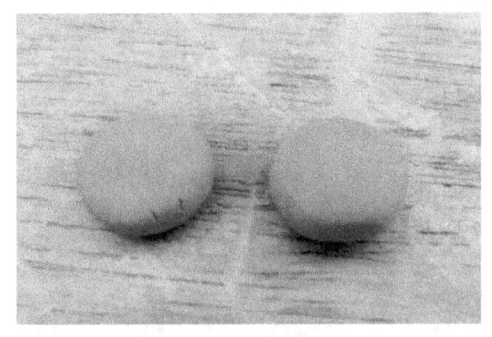

and then cut it in half, roll the two pieces into two small balls and squash them in the palm of one hand with the thumb of the other hand, check that they are the same size before you fit them to the pig's head.

To fit the ears crosshatch two patches immediately above the eyes and also crosshatch the two discs where the ears will attach to the pig.

Create slip in the crosshatch marks on the body and on the ears and press the ears firmly into the slip on

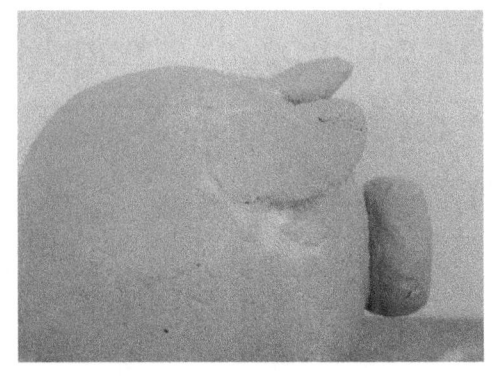 the head, again supporting the body in you palm. Complete this activity by smoothing the ears onto the head, blending the edge of the ears into the head helps to make a much more solid attachment to the body.

Make and fit the legs.

Take the clay in the palms of your hands and roll it onto a sausage shape, try to maintain a uniform thickness along the length of the sausage shape. Check the length against the template and finally tidy up the ends by tapping the sausage shape on the work surface.

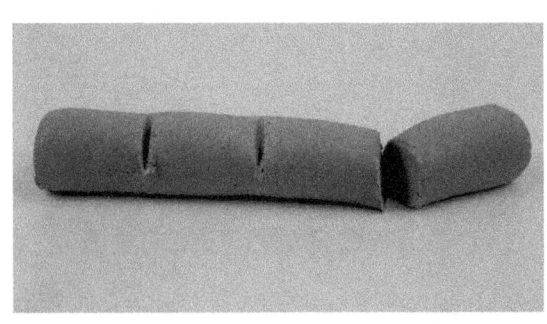 Mark the clay in three places in order to make four legs of the same length, cut the clay cleanly once you are satisfied that the marks are evenly spaced. Reshape the legs into cylindrical forms and crosshatch one end of each leg as shown in the next picture.

Crosshatch the underside of the pig's body in the places where the legs are to be fitted. The positioning is shown on the picture.

Create slip on the body and on each leg by rubbing water into the crosshatch marks with the brush.

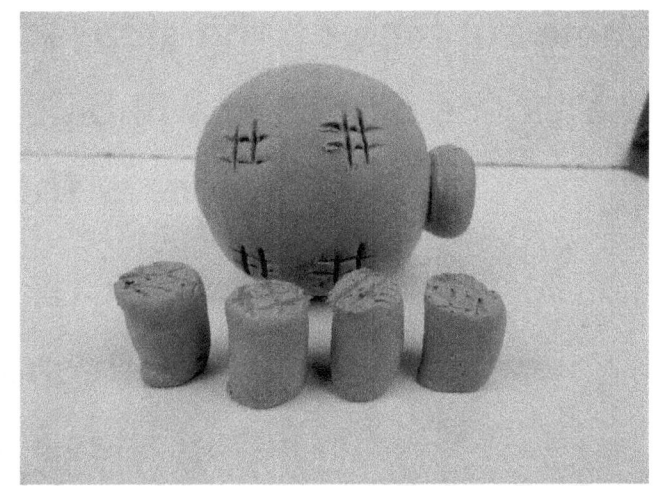

In order to prevent distortion in the ball of clay support the body in the palm of one hand while you press and twist the legs into poition.

Make and fit the tail.

Roll the clay ito a short, thin sausage shape to form the tail, create a patch of slip on the spot where the tail is to attach and also along the length of the tail.

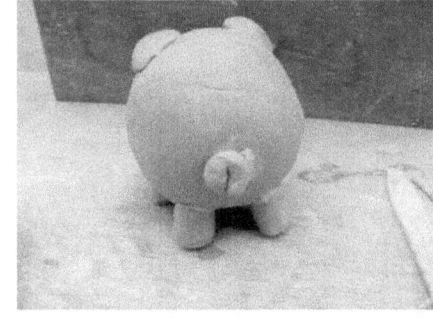

Press one end of the tail into the body and twist the tial round between thumb and finger and press the curly tail into the patch of slip on the body.

Make the base and fit the pig.

Prepare the clay by rolling it into a ball, then squash it as shown in the picture, roughly into the size and shape of the pancake shape which you need. Try to ensure that the thickness is the same across the whole surface of the slab. If it is too thick in places the figure attached will be sloping. If it is too thin in parts the piece will be weak.

Mark the base where the feet touch and make crosshatch areas in these positions.

Crosshatch the ends of the legs and make slip on the base and on the legs. Place the ends of the legs onto the base and taking leg by leg press each one in turn onto the base.

Use the pointed stick to make the pig's eyes and nostrils and cut the mouth into the snout using the edge of the knife. You can support the body in the palm of one hand while you are creating your pig's face. Add the cloven hoof detail with the knife point.

B. & M. Potterycrafts.

Thumb pot pig worksheet.

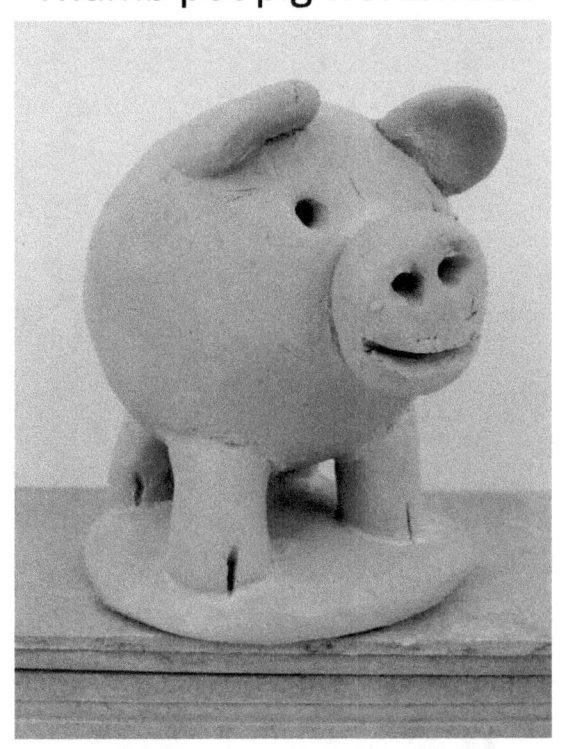

Clay.

Legs.   30 grams. 8 cms.

Snout.   10 grams.

Ears.   8 grams.

Body.   100 grams x 2.

Tail.   2 grams.

Base.   70 grams.

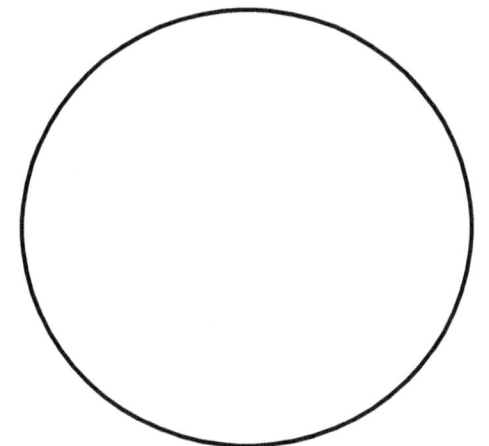